Your Project Mentor

Laverne Bennett

Published by Amz Marketing Hub

Editing through Reedsy by Elanor Harris

Acknowledgement: The author acknowledges study, and professional use of PRINCE2® is a (registered) Trade Mark of Axelos Limited. All rights reserved; PRINCE2 Agile® is a (registered) Trade Mark of Axelos Limited. All rights reserved; MSP® is a (registered) Trade Mark of Axelos Limited. All rights reserved; APM Body of Knowledge®, Association for Project Management incorporated by Royal Charter RC000890 and a registered charity No: 1171112. All rights reserved.

Published in Great Britain

Thanks to colleagues throughout my career who have guided the way through the good, and the challenging.

Those willing to keep on learning.

Those willing to share their time.

Table of Contents

Introduction

Does anyone really aspire to be a project professional when they are 18 years old?

I'd guess that unless that young adult knew one within the family, the option to be a delivery expert would likely not occur to them.

This book is to substitute for the family member you never had! It aims to provide personal views and insights with practical examples of projects, the people involved in specific roles, and, importantly, how projects could be kept under control and on the road to delivery. Its content is based on more than twenty years of experience utilising project, programme and portfolio methods and negotiating with human beings to get things done.

You're here, so you must be curious.

I won't lie; project environments are not for everyone. Continue reading to discover for yourself if you identify with the scenarios provided and get the project delivery buzz.

Chapter 1
Some Basics

Describing the delivery of projects to a newcomer can actually be boiled down to three key points:

- Knowing what is meant to be achieved (in detail)
- Knowing who you need to complete the work
- Knowing how to manage a project—especially when things go wrong

What is meant to be achieved

Let's get some terminology out of the way. Projects are a vehicle for time- and goal-focused achievement. They are started based on a list of objectives; these are the *scope* and should be agreed upon by all parties who will use or be affected by the result. A *project environment* is temporary; it's a bringing together of specific people and skill sets to achieve something, and when it's time to stop or complete the project, the environment is dissolved. Everyone moves on, some to other projects or their day job.

Simple example: The repainted sitting room

Two flatmates decide to repaint the sitting room. Flatmate A will be away for work and says it would be great if the walls were a relaxing pastel colour. Flatmate B goes out, buys pastel pink paint, and proceeds to paint two of the four walls. Later that day, he sends a photo of the whole room to Flatmate B, who questions the colour and which walls were painted—and the bill for his part of the £200 worth of paint!

The project scope could be:

Buying the paint, painting the walls

OR

Choosing the paint colours and finish (specific preferences from both flatmates), budget set, sample spot applied on each wall, deciding together on final colour, finish and on which walls it will be applied, who will paint the walls and by when.

Complex example: The new IT system

Marketing needs a way to track their customer relationships and ask senior management for an IT system. There may be many on the market. Marketing lists explicitly what they need it for, what they are interested in keeping as data, and how it will benefit their team objectives. These *requirements* are shared with IT system companies to find the best tool that matches. *Time* needed to complete specific things or the whole project and the *cost* or budget of the system work may or may not have been noted as decisions but verbally assumed as agreed. The project scope needs to be agreed upon by all teams or individuals invested in it being a success. These are the *stakeholders.*

The project scope could be:

Buying the system, installing it

OR

Buying the system, installing it, testing it, training users, communicating to everyone that it exists, who will use it, and why it's there

OR

Either of these with several people's interpretations layered on top—"I thought we were testing it to see it works, not that it couldn't be hacked into?" "I thought that the marketing data would be available to create flyers before the conference next month?"; "I thought our team would receive training because the technical repair team also meets customers."

These kinds of questions can be a nightmare to sort through and are referred to as *scope creep*. It occurs because a great idea is often seized upon for 'couldn't we' or 'aren't we also considering'.

Summary: The clearer the project scope is at the beginning, the easier it is to understand and control:

- The cost of the work
- What the planned work needs to be
- Who is needed (skills and knowledge)
- How long it will take
- What could go wrong—also known as the *risks*
- What actually does go wrong—these are *issues*
- What to do if there are permitted *changes* to the scope after the project work has already started

Take as much time as permitted to get this right. This will save you from potential late nights and fractured stakeholder relationships. Achieving the required scope means the result will be of appropriately agreed *quality.*

Who you need to complete the work

Be under no illusion. A project *plan* of things to be done or *tasks* can be fully mapped out, but that is not what delivers the result. Skilled humans, not plans, deliver projects. It is the relationships that the project professional builds with individuals who are scheduled to do specific tasks in the plan that actually make progress happen! A fully executable plan with correctly identified skilled individuals to match each task will ensure the right people are within a project team.

<u>Simple example: The repainted sitting room</u>

Flatmates A and B have decided to hire a painter to complete the redecorating. Flatmate A has had three different painters view and quote for the work; the chosen contractor is EconoPainters, as they fit the agreed budget and availability to start work on Friday. Flatmate A leaves for a week-long work conference. A note is left for Flatmate B with the mobile number, and an update about EconoPainters coming on Friday. It is Wednesday, and Flatmate B assumes without hesitation that it is this Friday. EconoPainters don't show up. Flatmate B is puzzled and texts Flatmate A. The date was correct! Flatmate A contacts EconoPainters and discovers that they had double-booked the skilled painter *resource* to another painting job and did not realise. It turns out that the repainted sitting room project was noted on a sticky note that didn't make it into the EconoPainters work diary.

People are not perfect. Did either flatmate confirm with EconoPainters that they were coming on the scheduled date? EconoPainters were trusted to be organised when they were booked to repaint the sitting room and show up as expected.

Complex example: Software development

A developer team is working on a sequence of complex software development tasks which include writing code and verifying and checking it for dependencies. The project team and manager have planned weekly progress update meetings in which the developers report that they are progressing with the work and that it is in hand. After a few weeks, the deadline has approached to complete the software update and hand it over to the validation team. It turns out the software is not ready, and the code checks, which are iterative until successful, have been needed several times instead of the software successfully passing the first time. The validation team are delayed in their start as a result. Up to this point, the project manager has been reporting the project as on time but now must log an issue, which costs time and requires an additional resource budget for the teams involved. Developer resource is tied up longer on this project which means they cannot start working on their next scheduled project.

Were the progress team meetings working effectively? It appears not if the conversations did not expose the delay. Were the right questions asked to tease out any risks or issues emerging? Was the right skill set assigned to the project? Were the individuals in the team empathetic to project teammates? In any event, the team's commitment to report progress accurately was not fulfilled.

Summary: Take the time to get to know the individuals and teams from whom you are expecting work or involvement. Offer opportunities for them to get to know each other. Team building enables and facilitates an open and honest team environment where they can create trusting relationships. Collaborative individuals understand how they can help each other complete work as expected. This increases the chances that problems will be mentioned early and can be sorted most effectively.

How to manage a project

Plans have been mentioned, as well as risks, issues and changes. A project plan captures all the objectives, also called *deliverables,* within the larger objective or end result.

<u>Simple example: The repainted sitting room</u>

End result—repainted sitting room.

> Deliverable 1—the Requirements Document includes the decisions on budget, timescale and complexity expectation—a big redecoration or refresh.
>
> Deliverable 2—the Resource Plan includes the paint-purchasing decisions, the supplier/painting service quotation process and final selection completion.
>
> Deliverable 3—the Implementation Plan includes the skilled individuals appropriately assigned and timings incorporated for a smooth flow of work.

Deliverables are presented as nouns to ensure that activities are not busy-ness, but are instead aligned to achieving step changes as the project.

Activities are *tasks* that can be grouped into *milestones*; these are past-tense verb phrases. The culmination of completed milestones contributes to the achievement of each deliverable.

This means:

Deliverable A – Requirements document

Milestone 1 – Budget decided

Task 1.1 – Review of spare cash situation completed

Task 1.2– Agreement reached on budget and cost split

Milestone 2 – Timescale decided

Task 2.1 – Flatmates comparison of personal diary commitments completed

Task 2.2 – Flatmates comparison of work diary commitments completed

Task 2.3 – Agreement reached on when the work can take place (this would need to also take into account any cash flow *dependency* from Milestone 1)

Milestone 3 – Scale of work decided

Task 3.1 – Review of ideas and discussion completed

Task 3.2 – Prioritisation completed for the **must-haves** for the redecoration (to achieve the look desired)

Task 3.3 – Decision is made about how the flatmates will handle any time, cost or problems encountered

Deliverable B – Resource plan

Milestone 1 – Paint buying complete

Task 1.1 – Paint shops selected for visit and price comparisons

Task 1.2 – Decision made on which place to buy the paint from

Task 1.3 – Paint purchased

Milestone 2 - Supplier/painting service quotation process and selection completion

Task 2.1 – Painting job posted up on the Internet for expression of interest

Task 2.2 – Spoken to each painting company

Task 2.3 – In-person visits completed with short-listed painting companies

Task 2.4 – Quotations received from painting companies

Task 2.5 – Flatmates decision on the quotation to accept

Task 2.6 – Flatmates have fed back to the painting companies to confirm the booking of the winning company

Task 2.7 – Painting company response received to confirm the scheduled booking for the work

Deliverable C - Implementation plan

Milestone 1 – Preparation completed

Task 1.1 – Sitting room is prepared for painting

Milestone 2 – Painting completed

Task 2.1 – Painter's redecoration is completed

Task 2.2 – Flatmates' review of the quality of the work and feedback to the painters is completed

Milestone 3 – Completion of final tasks

Task 3.1– Invoice from the painters received

Task 3.2 – Sitting room put back into use

Task 3.3 – Invoice from the Painters has been paid

For simplicity, this rough plan generally includes or implies *assignees* or the responsible individuals to complete the task. Each task would need a start and finish date based on an anticipated length of time the task should take to finish; this is the *duration.* Every line item in a plan needs to be reported on through a *status,* this is a set list of descriptions which are selected to show the task progress in the plan. Common status categories include *New* (not started), *In progress, Pending Approval, Completed, and Cancelled.* A fully executable plan would be in a table with columns for Description (the deliverables, milestones, tasks), Assignee, Start date, Finish date, Duration, and Status. Please note that the term "task" in this paragraph is commonly used by project professionals as an umbrella term for deliverables, milestones and tasks themselves. Be mindful that when someone refers to a task, it may not be specific but an item in the Description column of the project plan.

Summary: It is important to recognise that a plan doesn't guarantee that everything will unfold exactly as outlined.

From the plan above, we can recognise that there are potentially some things which **could** happen to impact the whole project. These are *risks*. As we know from earlier, there is a risk that the supplier **may** not complete the work within the specified time, cost, or quality agreed upon. The impact **could** be that the work takes longer, costs more, or requires other decisions to maintain the level of quality that was asked.

When a risk actually happens, it becomes an *issue*. Both will require communications and decisions from stakeholders to bring the plan back on track or make a choice to *replan* the remaining work to incorporate the new *change*. Once the high-level stakeholders have approved a replanned project plan, it is established as the *baseline*. Imagine this as a new line in the sand to continue from. From that point on, the replanned plan (as was) is again referred to as the *plan.* Sorry about that. This process may repeat several times during a project, highlighting the importance of well-organised documentation and effective use of project *controls.*

Chapter 2
Staying in Control

Which house do you belong to?

Speak to any project professional, and you'll hear about *project methodology*. It's like belonging to a house at Hogwarts. There is a family allegiance to following a way of working through a project based on the training received. In the UK, APM and PRINCE2 are the leading methodologies. Both come with comprehensive *governance* structures and ways in which control can be applied at each *stage* or milestone within a project.

The commonalities across project methodologies include the following:

- A project *initiation* or start process including *roles* and responsibilities clearly defined and undertaken for clear decision making. These are the high-level *stakeholders*. Initiation defines the scope, time, cost, and quality to deliver the project. Additionally, the project must establish a clear understanding of the *success criteria* or what a good project outcome looks like.

- *Stages* in a project plan represent predetermined points in time where specific work is completed and defined scope objectives are achieved. These stages can vary in number, ranging from one to several, and upon completion of all stages, the project is considered finished.
- Reference and reverence to the triad of agreed Time, Cost and Quality.
- A need to have controls which encompass both tools and processes for effectively managing change.
- Strong processes for risk mitigation and issue resolution.
- A project *completion* or endpoint is reached when the scope and success criteria are achieved. Any exceptions need to be considered by high-level stakeholders who will decide whether they warrant a follow-up project or align with broader business objectives.
- A collection of l*essons* so we understand what went smoothly or where we encountered challenges. Why make the same mistake twice in similar projects!

Delivery paths

It's important to call out that methodologies can also be tailored to a specific approach to project *delivery*. This means the way in which the project tasks are completed in the broadest sense. As illustrated in Chapter 1, you'll recognise a kind of *waterfall* sequence where tasks logically flow from one to the next. Waterfall is a traditional delivery mechanism based on predefining what the result will be and having agreed-upon requirements. It relies on logical, chronological order, and practical dependencies, emphasising the importance of completing tasks in the right order. Tasks may or may not be related to each other, but overall, from top to bottom, the plan accumulates deliverable and milestone completions. By the end, the project is completed. It does allow for some tasks to happen at the same time, in *parallel*, as needed.

In Chapter 1, there was an example of software development. The incremental improvement of code quality, coupled with iterations of testing and recoding, lends itself to the principles of *Agile* or *Scrum sprint* methodologies.

<u>Simple example: Building a birdhouse</u>

Picture this: it is spring, and you are in your shed with the desire to build a birdhouse. You cut wood for the four walls (one with a hole bored in it), the base and the pitched roof, securing everything together with screws. You also add a nice perch. Proudly, you hang it on a lovely tree, where you can happily watch for new tenants. Quickly, you realise that the hole isn't big enough for the visiting birds. You take the house down and make the hole larger, hang the house back up again and eagerly await more *feedback*. While there is definite interest in the accommodation, you notice the perch is too short for the birds' wide bodies. The birds are unable to land properly to have a look inside. Taking the house back down again, you replace the perch with a longer and sturdier post.

Although the example may sound a bit counter-intuitive, the purpose is to illustrate the evolution of requirements through a concept called *failing fast*. The goal of this mini-project was to create a birdhouse. This was achieved, but the initial quality fell short. *Rework* was required to accommodate new information or *feedback* from *user testing*. This iterative approach unfolded in minutes or hours as opposed to the more extended two-week cycles typical in business project scrum sprints. Tasks are set out and assigned to an appropriately skilled resource. During that time, there is a continuous learning process from quick successes or failures. When the two-week sprint is nearing completion, an evaluation of the fit-for-purpose quality of the result occurs, leading to a revised set of work for the subsequent two-week sprint. This cycle continues until the desired quality is established. Agile delivery enables ongoing adaptation throughout the project, differing from Scrum, where there are no sprints. Agile or Scrum are often considered the preferred delivery paths over waterfall when time and cost are less of a *constraint* or limitation with a primary focus on the quality element of the project triad.

Summary: Delivery path approach is primarily chosen based on the most significant restriction. Is there limited time and or limited budget? Waterfall ensures a more consistent momentum towards agreed requirements. Is there more time, more budget? Then, perhaps agile or scrum sprints will provide a better result, especially if the requirements are more fluid and open to innovative discoveries during the production process.

Risk—OMG!

We deal with risk in our everyday lives. We do particular things or take specific actions to *mitigate* them. These actions aim to reduce the *likelihood,* or the chances of a risk happening, with *severity* that could hurt us.

Simple example: Crossing the street—at the kerb, there is a low risk of being hit by a car. Before you step off the pavement, you realise that the risk increases as soon as you step onto the street. The mitigation or action to limit impact (and, by now, your habit) is to look both ways before you step onto the street in order to cross. You are responsible for identifying, assessing and mitigating the risk. When reaching the other side of the road, there is an opportunity to reflect and learn lessons for future strolls.

Risk management involves conditional thinking. A multitude of things **could** occur during a project *lifecycle,* and it would be impractical to list all conceivable risks and expect an individual to mitigate all of them. Therefore, each risk is assigned a score ranging from one to five based on the likelihood multiplied by severity. This is referred to as the *RAG score* (Red, Amber, Green score). Once a mitigating action has taken place on a risk, there should be a reduction in the overall score. This is the *residual* RAG score.

RAG follows the logic of a traffic light:

Red indicates high likelihood and severity—STOP and take action immediately.

Amber indicates a moderate level of likelihood and severity, with one tending to be predominant—

PROCEED WITH CAUTION and consider taking appropriate action.

Green signifies a low likelihood and severity—REASONABLY SAFE to proceed, but monitor the risk going forward to see if any conditions change.

The full process for risk management within a project environment is:

- Identify the risk.
- Report the risk to the project manager or lead.
- Fact find about the risk generally and assign it to someone knowledgeable with an appropriate level of influence. This is a *risk owner.*
- The risk owner defines the mitigation and takes action.
- There is a regular review of the mitigation to see how effective it has been.
- Reporting the risk and its mitigation success to higher-level stakeholders.
- Monitor for any changes to the risk and escalate for further decisions on whether actions are still needed.
- If the risk is mitigated and managed, it can be *accepted* as unlikely to happen and will not go

away. We understand we will continue with project aims in spite of it.
- If the risk flares up or mitigations are not as effective as predicted, the risk may become an issue.

Summary: The key message for risks is OMG! They all need an Owner, Mitigations, and Good monitoring.

Issues need resolutions

So it's not a rumour; something factual has happened, and a specific impact is being experienced. Whether or not it was on the risk radar, what steps do you take within a project environment?

- Identify the issue (the sooner, the better!).
- Report it to the project manager or lead so it can be recorded
- Fact find for more information, then assign the issue to an owner who can actively participate and coordinate work.
- *Turn off the tap*. This means if the issue is ongoing and causing damage, this needs to be brought under control as quickly as possible, and impacts stopped. Take action as necessary. A good example is a hacker leaking personal data—turning off the tap is the

organisation closing all access doors and permissions to halt the hack.

- Convene a team of individuals who know about the issue and have the necessary skills, knowledge and influence to discover and understand how the issue occurred. This is conducting a *root cause analysis.*
- Agree on an action plan.
- Enact the plan and monitor the action completions—escalate if necessary.
- Report the situational progress to high-level stakeholders and leverage any influence to get the issue resolved quickly.
- Resolution implementation until the issue is successfully closed.

RAG scores are also used to record the initial issue. It has a definite impact, so the *likelihood* is a maximum of five. In contrast, the *severity* is dependent on the type of issue and volume of those affected. The initial multiplied score is required to inform the scale of transition, and mitigation required to have a residual score into the range of a green score.

Summary: While issues can be resolved, and the project can return to its plan, resolving them may have certain cost or time implications. The severity of these may require a replan. In this case, the project briefly pauses to regroup, assess the remaining tasks (time, resource booking, quality and deliverables) and amend the plan appropriately. Once the revised, baselined plan is in place, the project continues.

But what about change?

A *change* in project terms is a deviation from what was originally agreed, planned or budgeted for within the delivery timescale.

Whenever a project encounters

- Late scope requests that are agreed to be incorporated
- Time or cost impacts from risks or issues
- Forced replanning
- High-level stakeholder role changes
- Quality requirement changes

Change must be documented and accepted by high-level stakeholders. This document, often known as a Change Request should include a description of the change, its necessity, and the impacts it may have, and it'll require approval and sign-off from high-level stakeholders.

<ins>Summary:</ins> Changes are not the decision of a project manager or the project team but of those who have the strategic approval for delivery timescales, the budget or the business objective being enabled

through the project's end result. The project must have accurate records of every sanctioned change as this becomes the audit record against the original project scope and objectives.

Stop! The wheels have fallen off!

No one likes to consider or agree to end a project prematurely. However, it is important to remember that this is a viable course of action for the right reasons! Sometimes, the project scope grows unwieldy, and costs accumulate from isolated approvals to become more and more, causing delays as the planned delivery rolls on. Before you know it, three years have passed, there is an overspent budget in the millions, and the original aims of the project are unclear or forgotten. A project that is chosen to stop is *closed,* tying up any loose ends appropriately in agreement with customers and all stakeholders.

With every element of change, project professionals need to revisit the fundamental reason why the project exists. The *business case* itemises and contextualises a project and includes all the information we have previously discussed—scope, time, cost, quality, stakeholders, milestones, success criteria, and benefits. Project *benefits* are the improvements to the business as a whole expected as a result of project execution, with quantitative or qualitative value.

At the turning point of each Stage, high-level stakeholders should decide if the project can proceed. A comparison between the original business case and current project *reports* will indicate whether things are still looking positive to continue.

Are all changes approved? Yes.

Is the project still within budget? Yes.

Is it still in time for the approved plan? Yes.

Does it align with expected benefits and end-result deliverables? Yes.

If so, let's continue.

<u>Summary:</u> The questions here are not exhaustive but serve to illustrate the importance of regularly checking, confirming the project's position and reporting in a transparent way to high-level stakeholders. Project professionals need to demonstrate consistent integrity in recommendations to either continue or stop a project.

Chapter 3
Human beings

The most predictable element in projects is that humans will miscommunicate, misunderstand or get distracted. We all tend to fail at times. Knowing this enables project professionals to try and enable and facilitate relationships for success. After all, people performing together have fewer pronounced weaknesses when well-aligned in terms of working methods and personality, complemented by a strong team spirit and trust.

Project method is largely *hard* skills, applying guidance, tools and knowledge for project delivery. There is often less emphasis on *soft* skills, which focus on emotional intelligence, personal interactions and relationships, which play a pivotal role in achieving results. This section dedicates itself to defining roles and responsibilities while also addressing the nuanced aspect of managing people. The key takeaway is that good project professionals are not driven by bureaucracy; instead, they must cultivate emotional intelligence and adaptable skills to negotiate delivery collaboratively.

Project roles

Up until now, the terms 'project professionals' and 'high-level stakeholders' have been used generally to describe roles.

Project professionals, serving as the individuals leading the project, may carry titles such as project manager, project lead, associate project manager, associate project lead, delivery lead, and project coordinator. Their role, irrespective of title, is to lead, manage, and coordinate the project team, execute the project plan and make everything happen. Project professionals are responsible for resource planning, risk and issue management, and reporting upwards. They do not make decisions but rather foster discussions for options and provide recommendations for a decision to be made by the Sponsor.

High-level stakeholders in practice include (in the broadest sense):

- Sponsor—the champion and owner of the project, advocating for it at the highest business level. The sponsor is empowered to make decisions to keep the project achieving completion. Primary sign-off on change documentation.
- Internal stakeholders such as Users—individuals or groups involved in

requirements gathering, as the project is intended to be used by them for a specific benefit to the overall company. They offer a relevant voice and opinion for the decisions required.

- External stakeholders such as Customers, Suppliers, Contractors, and Shareholders are individuals appointed as appropriate to the project business case to ensure that there is an appropriate voice and opinion for any decisions required.

These high-level stakeholders collectively form a Project Board and the decision-making body for recommendations brought forward.

Project delivery involves a group of task assignees called the Project Team or Working Group. Task assignees are selected for their knowledge and skillset or because they are the *subject matter experts* (SMEs) in the company. Membership could also include Change Management, Communications and Project Management Office representatives. This group commits to share emerging risks or issues during the project lifecycle. The project professional leads this group to work collaboratively towards achieving the project aims.

Herding cats

Project professionals have a responsibility to ensure that the project plan is executed. This means assigning tasks, ensuring they are started and completed, and that any risks or issues that could halt progress are controlled. Think of them as conductors for a large orchestra, except each part of the orchestra has competing priorities, time pressures, or unknown considerations that could jeopardise the work being done. Enter the cat analogy. Unlike the dog, who is at the beck and call of its owner and compliant, the cat has its own will, competing priorities which they keep to themselves, and a seemingly aloof demeanour.

A project team works best when all members understand their role in the team, what they are delivering in the plan, and who is dependent on them within the team to get it done. The fostering of interdependent interactions is critical for task completion and healthy disclosure of any problems as soon as possible. To this end, project professionals dedicate considerable time to chasing project team members for task completions, providing reminders, offering and assisting with any rough patches encountered during tasks, and also, perhaps most importantly, building and smoothing relationships within the team and with external stakeholders.

Coordinating and delegating work to individuals to whom you are not the line manager (and having them completed) is called *matrix management*. This is the essence of cat herding. It is a skill set in its own right, and striking a balance with each individual who will have their own needs, interests or investments in completing or not completing assigned tasks is vital. Project professionals who invest in understanding their team members and matrix management gain a significant advantage.

On a formal level, project professionals need to master the art of chairing a meeting, which is essential for regular project team meetings, risk or issue meetings, or any ad hoc meetings required to iron out concerns and keep work progressing.

In order to chair a meeting effectively, there are a few key points which must be straight in your mind before you begin:

- Objective or aim for the meeting.
- Do you have knowledgeable individuals in the room/on the call to enable the aim to be met (if so, then the meeting is *quorate*)?
- How you plan to organise the conversation, or what approach to the activities you will utilise to enable the group to come to the outcome that you or the group need from the session.

- How you will ensure all participants have the safe space and consideration to contribute their views to the conversation.

There should be a recap at the end of the meeting of the key actions taken (including to whom they are assigned and by when they need to be completed) as well as a written record of the meeting (the minutes), and any follow-on meeting to be scheduled.

There are many situational tips and tricks available to coordinate your team (herd the cats!). These can be different depending on your team members, so you may wish to research this further under topics such as body language, team building, and conflict resolution.

Managing upwards

The project professional serves as the key liaison upwards to the Sponsor and Project Board, and downwards to the Project Team. While the matrix management of project team members may be more (relatively) comfortable or relatable, matrix management upwards is nuanced. Coordinating a high-level stakeholder to complete a task or take forward a topic to champion with their peers (so assigned work can continue at the project team level) may be tricky. A consideration to apply is the *circle of influence* of the respective high-level stakeholder.

Everyone has a circle of influence. It can be thought of as the psychological and emotional realm that can influence those around them. The intention is not malicious or negative; rather, it acknowledges that someone you wish to influence might lack the time or information to understand the purpose of your request. It is not that you're arguing that it is a priority but that you are providing factual explanations about the current conditions and the perspectives of the project team so that there is a better understanding. If you are a project professional, then fostering a professional relationship with the Sponsor and Project Board members is essential. This will not only help to expand your circle of influence but also aid in helping them understand your work style and level of integrity. It builds trust both ways for successful project delivery.

When you approach a high-level stakeholder outside your circle of influence with a request, this is a new challenge. Consider your familiarity with them—how well do you know them? If not well, then identify someone within your circle of influence who is their peer. The idea of 'who you know' becomes pivotal in this scenario. Perhaps the stakeholder is someone you know in passing, and you just need their high-level peer to introduce you – adding credibility and respect to the new relationship. That helpful high-level stakeholder is known as an *advocate*. Advocates are important in facilitating connections between individuals while providing the project with representation in discussions where the Sponsor might be absent or inaccessible to the project professional.

Summary: Managing upwards hinges on some very important professional values: integrity, transparency, honesty, and respect. If you are starting your career, keep an eye out as you progress through different roles and interact with colleagues (peers or high-level stakeholders). What values do they live? Do you share them? What values do you find important in those you work with? Research professional values and the professional lives of people you look up to. Decide to make conscious decisions about what values you'd like to live and have others know you for.

Conclusion

If I had been asked at 20 years old what my longest career would be, I would not have predicted that I would be a project professional.

While this book has hopefully provided insight and practical examples of projects, the people and management of those involved in specific roles, and the criticality of controls to project delivery, it is, in fact, your gut which will inform you now of the useful information collected from this read.

Project professionals talk about gut feeling. If you've found this an interesting subject and the project method has a feel of logical, scalable tidiness to it, feel free to research further into the topics mentioned.

Projects are constantly taking place in all sectors and countries. This is no understatement.

Enjoy the journey, and keep learning!

Printed in Great Britain
by Amazon

58569534R00030